# The Great
# PRAYER
# AWAKENING
## *of 1857-58*

*The Prayer Movement That Ended
Slavery and Saved the American Union*

## Eddie L. Hyatt

HYATT PRESS * 2019

*The Great Prayer Awakening of 1857-58*
By Eddie L. Hyatt

© 2019 by Hyatt International Ministries, Incorporated
ALL RIGHTS RESERVED.
Published by Hyatt Press
A Subsidiary of Hyatt Int'l Ministries, Incorporated
*Mailing Address (2018)*
Hyatt Int'l Ministries
P.O. Box 3877
Grapevine, TX 76099-3877

*Internet Addresses*
Email:   dreddiehyatt@gmail.com
Web Site:  www.eddiehyatt.com
Social Media: Eddie L. Hyatt
Unless otherwise indicated, all Scripture quotations
are taken from the New Kings James Version of the Bible. ©
1979, 1980, 1982 by Thomas Nelson, Inc. Publishers.
ISBN: 978-1-888435-27-6
Printed in the United States of America

# Table of Contents

# Preface

America today seems hopelessly divided along political and cultural divides. Power hungry politicians, it seems, will stoop to any low to gain or retain power, including destroying the lives and reputations of their opponents.

College campuses have become centers of radical ideologies of cultural change with student groups often opposing with violence guest speakers with whom they, and their liberal professors, disagree. The angry rhetoric from all sides is crude, rude, threatening and revolting.

Perhaps at only one other time in history was America so deeply divided, and that was at the time of the Civil War. Such deep divisions have destroyed many nations and would have destroyed America at that time except for one overruling factor—the Great Prayer Awakening.

In 1857, four years before the outbreak of the Civil War, a great prayer revival swept unexpectedly across America. As if drawn by an invisible force, multitudes daily gathered in churches, halls, fire stations and auditoriums to pour out their hearts to God.

This prayer revival was timely, for the nation would soon pass through her darkest hour and would need the Divine assistance to survive. This great prayer revival released the spiritual and moral resources necessary to save the nation from total ruin.

This prayer revival was America's Third Great Awakening. The First Great Awakening gave birth to the nation as it ebbed and flowed between 1726 and 1770. The Second Great Awakening saved the nation from the negative influences of the French Revolution and the European Enlightenment and tamed the bawdy western frontier as it ebbed and flowed from around 1800-1840.

For any revival to be called a Great Awakening it should have the following three characteristics.

1. It is an obvious sovereign work God in that it has arisen apart from any identifiable human plan, strategy or design.
2. It is non-sectarian and touches people of all sects and denominations. No one group, or church, can "own" the revival
3. It is not localized or regional but has an obvious national impact on the nation and its culture.

The Great Prayer Awakening of 1857-58 possessed these characteristics, which is why I have chosen to call it America's "Third Great Awakening."

America is once again deeply divided and there is no answer to be found in politics, education or formal religion. There is, however, an answer.

The answer for America today is the same as when the First Continental Congress gathered for the first time on September 9, 1774 and opened their proceedings with prayer. It is the same as when George Washington, upon assuming command of the American Army, ordered that each day was to begin with prayer led by the commander of each unit.

It is the same answer Abraham Lincoln found at a very critical moment in the Civil War when General Robert E. Lee was marching into Pennsylvania with 76,000 troops. Lincoln later told how he got down on his knees and poured out his heart to God, and as he prayed, "A sweet comfort crept into my soul that God Almighty had taken the whole business into His own hands."

This book is sent forth with the prayer that it will be the means of awakening citizens of all political persuasions to the power of prayer. It is sent forth with the prayer that Christians in America will join Vice-President Mike Pence in taking seriously the promise of II Chronicles 7:14, which he often quotes. In fact, he purposely took the oath of office with His Bible opened to this passage. It reads,

> *If My people who are called by My name will humble themselves, and pray and seek My face, and turn from their wicked ways, then will I hear from heaven, and will forgive their sin and heal their land.*

# Chapter I

# America, Prayer & Slavery

*That it be recommended to all the United States, as soon as possible, to appoint a day of solemn fasting and humiliation; to implore of Almighty God the forgiveness of the many sins prevailing among all ranks, and to beg the assistance of his Providence in the prosecution of the present just and necessary war.* – Congressional Proclamation, Dec. 11, 1776

Prayer is not something unique or uncommon to the American experience. Prayer, so to speak, has been a part of America's national DNA from the time of the landing of the Jamestown settlers in 1607 and the Pilgrims in 1620.

But just because Christians pray does not mean they are perfect or godly. It does mean, however, that they acknowledge the Creator and their need of Him, and this acknowledgement makes them vulnerable and open to His workings in their lives.

## The Earliest Immigrants Prayed

Before the Jamestown settlers disembarked on April 29, 1607, their chaplain, Rev. Robert Hunt, designated a three-day period of prayer and repentance to prepare their hearts for dedicating the land of their new home to God. After the three days of prayer, Hunt then led the party to the wind-swept shore of Cape Henry where they erected a seven-foot oak cross, brought from England.

They then gathered around the cross to pray and give thanks to God for His mercy and grace in bringing them safely to this new land. In his dedicatory prayer, Hunt declared, "From these very shores the gospel shall go forth to not only this New World, but the entire world."[1]

Before departing Holland for the New World, the Pilgrims, set aside "a day of solemn humiliation" to seek the Lord's blessing and guidance before their departure on July 22, 1620. Both the Pilgrims and the Puritans who followed them set aside special days for prayer and fasting. At first, this was done in response to pressing needs, but eventually became a part of the culture of New England.

## The Founding Generation Prayed

The prayer tradition was very much alive during the Revolutionary War. Upon taking command of the bedraggled Colonial Army, General George Washington ordered that each day was to begin with prayer led by the commander of each unit. At the same time, the Continental Congresses issued no less than fifteen calls for days of prayer and fasting during the war. The proclamation for December 11, 1776, included the exhortation,

> That it be recommended to all the United States, as soon as possible, to appoint a day of solemn fasting and humiliation; to implore of Almighty God the forgiveness of the many sins prevailing

---

[1] Eddie Hyatt, *Pilgrims and Patriots* (Grapevine, TX: Hyatt Press, 2016), 56.

among all ranks, and to beg the assistance of his Providence in the prosecution of the present just and necessary war.[2]

This prayer tradition continued with presidents issuing proclamations for days of prayer. Washington, Adams, Jefferson, Madison, Jackson, Lincoln and others issued proclamations designating special days for the nation to pray and offer thanksgiving to God.

## Slavery & the Prayer Awakening

The brilliant black economist, Dr. Walter E. Williams, after pointing out that slavery has been practiced by numerous civilizations and peoples throughout recorded history, stated that the unique characteristic of slavery in America was the "moral outrage" against it. In an article entitled "How the Great Awakening Ended Slavery," I have shown that this "moral outrage" was a product of the First Great Awakening that transformed Colonial America and sensitized the consciences of many to this horrendous sin.

Nonetheless, despite the impact of the Awakening, the slavery issue was not settled at the nation's founding. For the most part, the Founders had come to abhor slavery, which is indicated by the fact that they outlawed slavery in the newly established Northwest Territory at the time they ratified the U.S. Constitution. Most Founders also took steps to disentangle themselves from the institution.

---

[2] Hyatt, *Pilgrims and Patriots*, 123.

However, out of concern that they could not form a successful union without the southern slave states, they left the issue to the discretion of the individual states already in existence and thereby left the matter for a later generation to resolve.

Nonetheless, although they did not abolish slavery, they were careful not to affirm the institution. In the founding documents, for example, the Founders avoided using the words "slave" and "slavery." Neither did they use the words "black" and "white." Instead of race classifications, the Founders spoke of "citizens," "persons," and "other persons."

Because the Founders were careful to avoid any classifications based on race, an opening was made for the argument that the rights guaranteed therein applied to all. This was obvious to abolitionists, like Frederick Douglas, and Civil Rights leaders, like Dr. Martin Luther King, Jr., who based their arguments for equal rights on America's founding documents.

Nonetheless, some of the Founders, such as George Mason, were disturbed by what they saw as a wrongful compromise with the southern states. Mason, who is called the "Father of the Bill of Rights," warned of Divine judgment if the slavery question was not settled then and there. He declared,

> Every master is born a petty tyrant. They bring the judgment of Heaven upon a country. As nations cannot be rewarded or punished in the next world, they must be in this. By an inevitable chain of

causes and effects, Providence punishes national sins by national calamities.[3]

Abraham Lincoln described this refusal of the Founders to acknowledge slavery in the Constitution as being like a man who hides an ugly, cancerous growth until the time comes that it can be eradicated from his body.

By the mid-19th century, it was obvious that the time for eradication had arrived, but the patient would require some spiritual anesthesia to survive the ordeal, and this is where the Great Prayer Awakening came into play.

## Judgement Mixed with Mercy

Many see the Civil War with its widespread destruction and excessive loss of life as the fulfillment of Mason's warning of judgement. Thomas Jefferson had issued a similar warning for it was in the context of the continuance of slavery in America that he warned,

> God who gave us life, gave us liberty. And can the liberties of a nation be thought secure when we have removed their only firm basis, a conviction in the minds of the people that these liberties are a gift from God? That they are not to be violated but with His wrath? Indeed, I tremble for my country when I reflect that God is just and that His justice cannot sleep forever.[4]

With this sort of Biblical and moral opposition to slavery at the nation's founding, it is easy to see how its days were

---

[3] Hyatt, *Pilgrims and Patriots*, 160.
[4] Hyatt, *Pilgrims and Patriots*, 160-61.

already numbered. This is the "moral outrage" that Williams referred to. One can only wonder if the Founders had dealt with slavery at the birth of the nation, if perhaps the apocalyptic devastation of the Civil War could have been avoided.

And while we may see the Civil War as God's judgement on the nation for its institutional sin of slavery, we may also see the Prayer Revival as an act of Divine mercy in which God gave the nation the spiritual resources needed to survive the calamity. God's mercy in the Prayer Revival also resulted in thousands being swept into the kingdom who shortly thereafter lost their lives in the war.

Abraham Lincoln recognized this dual outpouring of judgment and mercy on the land. In his 1863 proclamation for a day of prayer and repentance, he acknowledged that God, "While dealing with us in anger for our sins, hath nevertheless remembered mercy."

As America faces a host of new and different challenges in the 21st century, the Great Prayer Awakening of 1857-58 can shed light on our path and be a roadmap showing us the way forward in these times of great turmoil and distress.

# Chapter 2

# Why America Needed Revival in 1850

*The need for another awakening was great. By 1845, the "aftershocks" of the Second Great Awakening had subsided. A low, lax state of religious feeling prevailed. Outward religion was still practiced, but the earlier power and vitality was gone.* – Anonymous Writer

As the year 1857 dawned, moral apathy and spiritual indifference were gripping the American populace. Although a smattering of local revivals still occurred, the Second Great Awakening had run its course and a widespread religious indifference seemed to permeate all segments of society.

Some attributed the spiritual decline, at least in part, to an unhealthy preoccupation with the acquisition of wealth. After an economic crash in 1837, an economic boon ensued, fueled in part by the discovery of gold in California. One writer declared, "Men forgot God in pursuit of gold."[5]

## Disillusioned by Bad Theology

In addition, many had become spiritually disillusioned when one of the most popular preachers of the day, William Miller, proved to be wrong about his prediction

---

[5] Malcolm McDow & Alvin L. Reid, *FireFall* (Nashville: Broadman & Holman, 1997), 252.

that Christ would return on March 21, 1843. Thousands had been convinced by Miller's spellbinding expositions of Revelation and Daniel, so much so that newspapers reported people gathering on hill tops, some wrapped in "ascension robes," waiting for the Lord to catch them away on that day.

When March 21 passed without incident, Miller emerged a few days later with a new date for the Lord's return. Claiming he had made a slight error in his calculations, he reset the date for October 22, 1844.

When that day also passed without incident some, in utter disgust, totally abandoned their faith. Many others, while not abandoning their faith, slipped into a state of indifference and skepticism.

## Revival Turned into a Human Enterprise

Adding to the religious disillusionment and spiritual indifference was the fact that many had been turned off by the professionalizing of revival into a mere human enterprise. This had begun with Charles Finney's declaration that revival was no more a miracle than a crop of wheat, and his insistence on the use of the "proper means" to promote a revival.

Finney's emphasis had been appropriate in the context of the hyper-Calvinism he had faced; but later revivalists, lacking his gifts and commitment to truth, took his emphasis to the extreme and turned revival into a mere human enterprise.

13

This preoccupation with human devices and techniques to produce revival is seen in the statement of a "revivalist" that was quoted in the *Independent* in 1854. He brashly announced,

> Brethren, if you will follow the above directions for two months, and do not enjoy a revival of religion of the old stamp, you may tell me in public that I am no prophet.[6]

It was this human-centered approach to "revival" that caused R. A. Torrey, a generation later, to declare;

> We frequently have religious excitements and enthusiasm gotten up by the cunning methods and hypnotic influence of the mere professional evangelist or "revivalist," but these are not Revivals, and are not needed: they are a curse and not a blessing; they are the devil's imitation of a Revival.[7]

This mechanical, formulaic approach to revival and the extremes it produced only served to exacerbate public cynicism that was already running rampant. One writer said that by 1857, "The churches were sliding downhill." Another writer said;

> The need for another awakening was great. By 1845, the "aftershocks" of the Second Great Awakening had subsided. A low, lax state of religious feeling prevailed. Outward religion was still practiced, but the earlier power and vitality

[6] McDow & Reid, *FireFall*, 253-54.
[7] Eddie Hyatt, *Revival Fire* (Tulsa, OK: Hyatt Press, 2000), 112.

was gone. New immigrants were pouring into New York City at the rate of 1800 per day. Many of them were bringing with them the revolutionary atheism of Europe and were ignorant of America's spiritual history. The famous evangelist, Charles Finney, was still alive, but the sensation he had created in the 1820s and 1830s was a distant memory.[8]

## The Fight Over Slavery

Perhaps the greatest turmoil at this time was the growing moral outrage concerning slavery. Emotions ran high, not only politically, but also in the church. Many Southerners defended slavery with supposed Biblical arguments, saying it was God's way of saving the Africans who otherwise would perish in the spiritual darkness of their homeland. Some even quoted Paul's admonitions for slaves to obey their masters as justification for the institution. Others took a "softer" approach and argued that slavery was a secular topic that the church should not address directly.

Northern Christians tended to reject both approaches pointing out that the institution itself was contrary to the spirit and teachings of Jesus and the New Testament. Finney, who was an ardent abolitionist as well as a revivalist, declared that it was impossible to be on the right side of God and on the wrong side of the slavery issue and thus challenged the Christianity of those who

---

[8]

http://www.voiceoftheevangelists.com/Articles/HistoryofEvangelism/T HEGREATPRAYERREVIVALOF185758/tabid/466/Default.aspx defended the practice. His convert, Timothy Weld, became a leading abolitionist and worked equally hard to both convert sinners and end slavery.[9]

The conflict over slavery intensified and eventually led to entire denominations dividing over the issue. In 1837, for example, the Presbyterian Church divided between the pro-slavery and anti-slavery forces in its midst. During the mid-1840s the Methodist and the Baptist churches both divided over the slavery issue. These divisions, although painful and sad, were merely reflections of the deep divisions that were taking place politically and socially in the nation.

The intensity of the controversy increased evoking threats and sabre rattling by those on both sides of the issue and dampening spiritual impulses. One writer said, "As the nation drifted inexorably toward war, the thrust of American thought became almost entirely political and secular."[10]

---

[9] See Dr. Timothy Smith, *Revivalism and Social Reform in Mid-Nineteenth Century America*, who shows that modern civil rights movements have their roots in American revivalism.

[10] Vinson Synan, *The Holiness-Pentecostal Movement in the United States* (Grand Rapids: Eerdmans, 1971), 32.

# Chapter 3

# Humble Beginnings

*This was the winter of 1857 and 58, and it will be remembered that it was at this time that a great revival prevailed throughout all the northern states. Daily prayer meetings were established, and a divine influence seemed to pervade the whole land.* – Charles G. Finney

Jeremiah Lanphier, a forty-six-year-old layman and home missionary with the Dutch Reformed Church, trudged through the streets of the New York City day after day handing out gospel handbills and talking to people about the Savior. After three months of diligent outreach, he noted that the initial excitement he had once known was wearing thin as week after week he encountered indifference, and at times, outright rejection and opposition.

He had been hired by the Old Dutch North Church on Fulton Street in Manhattan to reach out to the many new immigrant families and businesses that were pouring into the area. Most of these immigrants knew little or nothing of a vital, heart Christianity, nor did they know anything of America's Christian origins.

Other churches had moved out of the area because of the demographic change, but the Fulton Street Church decided to remain and hire a home missionary to visit the new families and businesses. They chose Lanphier, a devout businessman, but with no experience in church and visitation work.

Lanphier diligently carried out his duties but experienced much discouragement with the spiritual indifference he encountered day after day. One day while carrying out his duties the thought occurred to him to host a prayer meeting during the noon hour when the business people would be on their lunch break.

## The Emphasis Shifts to Prayer

After much prayer, he decided to establish such a prayer meeting. His vision was to see business people come and pray for the unconverted during their lunch break from 12 noon to 1 P.M. People were welcome to attend for a few minutes or for the entire hour

The church gave him use of a lecture hall on the third floor of the church building and he advertised the prayer meeting by placing handbills in offices and warehouses in the area and posting one on the door of the church.

At the first prayer meeting on September 23, 1857, Lanphier prayed alone for the first half hour. Presently he heard footsteps on the stairs and a local businessman joined him. Before the meeting concluded at 1 p.m., four more arrived making a total of six from four different denominations.

At the next prayer meeting, the following Wednesday, twenty were present and the following week there were forty. The prayer times were accompanied with such blessing that they decided to make it a daily event and one week later over one-hundred attended the noon prayer meeting.

That very week the city and the nation were staggered by the worst economic crash in American history. Numerous banks closed, businesses closed, and many people lost their jobs. It resulted in many families scraping to just get by and put food on the table.

This, no doubt, helped fuel the growth, but it should be noted that the revival had already begun when this crash occurred. It should also be noted that the revival continued to grow and expand even after the economy recovered in just a few short months.

## A Simple, Punctual Format

The format of the prayer meeting was simple. At 12 noon the leader of the meeting would open with one or two verses of a well-known hymn, an opening prayer and then read any prayer requests. Anyone was then free to pray, share a prayer request or give a testimony.

No one was to take more than five minutes and if anyone took more than their allotted time the leader would ring a bell signaling for that person to conclude their prayer or comments.

The emphasis of the meeting was on the conversion of the lost and most of the prayers were directed to that end. Promptly at 1 p.m., the meeting was dismissed with a concluding prayer by the leader or someone appointed by him.

# God's Power is Manifest

Although very punctual and simple in format, the meetings were accompanied with great spiritual power. An overwhelming sense of God's presence seemed to pervade the very atmosphere and marvelous answers to prayer began to occur. As if drawn by an invisible force, people began to come from all parts of the city to be in the prayer meeting.

Not only Christians, but nonbelievers were drawn into the meetings, with many finding Christ during the times of prayer. One notorious criminal nicknamed "Awful Gardiner" came into the meeting and was gloriously saved and transformed. This created a further sensation and news of the prayer meeting spread throughout the city and beyond.

During another meeting, a man wandered in who intended to murder a woman and then commit suicide. He listened as someone was delivering a fervent exhortation and urging the duty of repentance. Suddenly the would-be murderer startled everyone by crying out, "Oh! What shall I do to be saved!" Just then another man arose, and with tears streaming down his cheeks asked the meeting to sing the hymn, "Rock of Ages, Cleft for Me." Both men were converted on the spot.[11]

The single room soon overflowed with both men and women now attending. Area pastors also began to attend and soon two adjoining rooms were also filled, with standing room only.

---

[11] "Revival Born in a Prayer Meeting," *Knowing & Doing*, Fall 2004.

Seeing the intense spiritual hunger and the need for more space, many pastors began opening their churches for morning and evening prayer and were astounded when their sanctuaries were filled with hungry seekers desiring to call on the name of the Lord.

## A Spirit of Prayer is Unleashed on the Nation

A spirit of prayer seemed to be unleashed from the Fulton Street meeting to the nation. Prayer meetings began springing up in Philadelphia, Boston, Washington D.C., Pittsburg, Cincinnati, Indianapolis, Chicago and in a multitude of smaller cities and rural areas.

People across the nation crowded into churches, fire stations, lodges and halls to pour out their hearts to God in prayer. It seemed that God Himself was gathering the people to prepare them for the dark and terrible night that was looming.

Amazing answers to prayer multiplied. It was not uncommon for parents to receive letters from a son or daughter telling how they had received Christ. When the parent would look at his/her journal, the day their child received Christ would be the same day they had turned in the prayer request.

Prayer gatherings in different cities began to communicate with one another and share reports of what God was doing in their midst. As these were read publicly, it caused great rejoicing and a sense that God was truly at work throughout the land. To cite one example, the New York City prayer gathering received the following wire from Philadelphia.

> To Mr. W. Wetmore, Fulton Street Meeting:
> Jayne's Hall Daily Prayer Meeting is crowded, upwards of three thousand present; with one mind and heart they glorify our Father in heaven, for the mighty work he is doing in our city and country in the building up of saints and the conversion of sinners. The Lord hath done great things for us, whence joy to us is brought.
> George H. Stuart, Chairman of the Meeting.[12]

Finney told of a prayer meeting in Boston in which a man stood and declared that he had just travelled almost two thousand miles from Omaha, Nebraska and had found "a continuous prayer meeting all the way."[13]

People preferred prayer meetings to conventional church services where preaching was the focal point of the gathering. Finney said that the general impression seemed to be, "We have had instruction until we are hardened; it is time for us to pray."[14]

The revival so captured the attention of the public that newspapers considered it to be front-page news, with headlines such as the following:

New Haven, CN—City's Biggest Church Packed Twice Daily for Prayer.

---

[12] Dr. Billye Brim, *First of All & the Awakenings* (Joplin, MO: Billye Brim Ministries, 2017), 122.
[13] Charles G. Finney, *An Autobiography* (Old Tappan, NJ: Oberlin College, 1908), 443.
[14] Finney, *An Autobiography*, 444.

Bethel, CN—Business Shuts Down for Hour Each Day; Everybody Prays.

Albany, NY—State Legislators Get Down on Knees.

Schenectady, NY—Ice on the Mohawk Broken for Baptisms.

Newark, NJ—Firemen's Meeting Attracts 2,000.

Washington, D.C.—Five Prayer Meetings Go Round the Clock.

New Haven, CN—Revival Sweeps Yale.

## People Gripped by Holy Spirit Conviction

The prayer meetings were characterized by a solemn sense of God's presence and much convicting power. Sinners seemed helpless in God's presence as the arrows of the Almighty pierced their hearts.

For example, in a noon prayer meeting at a church in downtown Kalamazoo, Michigan, the sanctuary was crowded with a standing-room-only crowd when a prayer request was read from a wife asking prayer for her unsaved husband.

Immediately, a man stood to his feet and with tears exclaimed, "I am that man. My wife is a good Christian woman and she must have sent that request. Please pray for me." He sat down and immediately a man in another part of the house stood to his feet weeping, and as if he had not heard the first man, declared, "That was my wife who sent that request. She is a good Christian woman and I have treated her badly. Please pray for me!" He sat down and another man stood, also convinced that it was his wife who sent the prayer request and after him a fourth and a fifth with similar confessions.

In a church in the Midwest twenty-five women got together once a week to pray for their unconverted husbands. As a result, the husbands came under the convicting power of the Holy Spirit and began coming to Christ. Shortly thereafter, the pastor traveled to the Fulton Street meeting and testified that on the Sunday he had left, the last of the twenty-five husbands had been converted and received into the church.

Four young sailors began a prayer meeting on the battleship, the North Carolina, which was docked in New York Harbor, serving as a receiving ship for the navy. Crewmen from different ships changed their assignment through this ship.

As the four young men prayed night after night, revival suddenly erupted as God's presence filled the ship and powerful conviction gripped the hearts and minds of all on board. Night after night sailors bowed humbly before the Lord and with tears of repentance called on His name. Hundreds were converted. Many were afterwards transferred to other ships and revival fires were kindled wherever they went.

One writer described a "zone of heavenly influence" that pervaded the eastern seaboard, extending out into the Atlantic and impacting the passengers and crews of approaching ships. He wrote,

> Revival began aboard one ship before it reached
> the coast. People on board began to feel the

presence of God and the sense of their own sinfulness. The Holy Spirit convicted them and they began to pray. As the ship neared the harbor, the captain signaled, "Send a minister." Another small commercial ship arrived in port with the captain, and every member of the crew converted in the last 150 miles. Ship after ship arrived with the same story: both passengers and crew were suddenly convicted of sin and turned to Christ before they reached the American coast.[15]

## The Nation is Awakened

A young D. L. Moody attended daily prayer meetings in Chicago and wrote to his mother, "Oh, how I do enjoy it! It seems as if God were here Himself."[16] In Washington D.C., Presidents Pierce (1853-57) and Buchannan (1857-61) attended prayer meetings that were organized in that city.

In Charleston, South Carolina, the black pastor of the Anson Street Presbyterian Church, John Giardeau, established a prayer meeting in 1858. He exhorted his congregation, comprised primarily of slaves, to pray and "wait for the outpouring of the Holy Spirit."

The prayer service grew until the auditorium was overflowing with more than two thousand people. As on the Day of Pentecost, the Holy Spirit suddenly fell upon those at the Anson Street Church.

---

[15] www.truthkeepers.com/prayer.html.
[16] McDow & Reid, *FireFall*, 266.

They began to sob, softly, like the falling of rain; then, with deeper emotion, to weep bitterly, or to rejoice loudly, according to their circumstances. It was midnight before he could dismiss the congregation. The meeting went on night and day for weeks. Large numbers of both black and white were converted and joined churches in the city.[17]

Finney described 1857-58 as a time when "a divine influence seemed to pervade the whole land."[18] He estimated that at the height of the revival fifty-thousand were being converted in a single week—and that without the aid of modern communication and technology.

Conservative estimates place the total number of conversions at around one million, but some have suggested that as many as two million may have been converted. The March 1858 issue of a religious journal reported,

> The large cities and towns from Maine to California are sharing in this great and glorious work. There is hardly a village or town to be found where 'a special divine power' does not appear displayed.[19]

Bishop McIlvaine, Chaplain of the U.S. Senate, in his annual address before the Diocesan Convention of Ohio in 1858, said,

---

[17] McDow & Reid, *FireFall*, 263.
[18] Finney, *An Autobiography*, 444.
[19] http://www.praywithchrist.org/prayer/layman.php.

I rejoice in the decided conviction that it [the Prayer Awakening] is the Lord's doing, unaccountable by any natural causes, entirely above and beyond what any human device or power could produce; an outpouring of the Spirit of God upon God's people, quickening them to greater earnestness in His service; and upon the unconverted, to make them new creatures in Christ Jesus.

# Chapter 4

# The Revival Spreads & Deepens

*I went out at midnight near my boarding-house and could distinctly hear the voice of prayer in the houses, in the barns, in the fields, in the streets. -* A.B. Earle, Canadian, Baptist Evangelist

The revival spilled over the northern border into Canada where powerful awakenings began to occur. Revival also erupted across the ocean in Ireland, Scotland and England. A common spirit of prayer characterized the revival wherever it appeared.

## Prayer Revival in Canada

Prayer meetings were begun in Hamilton, Ontario when Phoebe Palmer and her husband, Walter, visited that city in the fall of 1857. As in the Fulton Street meeting, a spirit of prayer gripped the hearts of the people. The November 5, 1857 issue of the *New York Christian Advocate and Journal* reported on this "Revival Extraordinary," saying,

> The work is taking its range with persons of all classes. Men of low degree and men of high estate for wealth and position; old men and maidens, and even little children, can be seen humbly kneeling together, pleading for grace. The mayor of the city, with other persons of like position, are not ashamed to be seen bowed at the altar of prayer beside the humble servant.[20]

---

[20] http://smithworks.org/revival/1857.html.

The following year, in 1858, A. B. Earle, a Baptist evangelist, reported that he was one of five ministers baptizing new believers simultaneously because of the massive numbers. Concerning the awakening in one Canadian village, Earle wrote,

> I went out at midnight near my boarding-house and could distinctly hear the voice of prayer in the houses, in the barns, in the fields, in the streets.[21]

## Ireland & the UK are Impacted

Prayer Revival also erupted in Ireland and the British Isles. A small group in Ireland began meeting for prayer in September of 1857, at the very same time Lanphier was beginning the prayer meeting in New York City. This prayer meeting soon grew to fifty and ignited a revival that spread across the country over the next two years.

Then in August of 1858 two Presbyterian ministers from Ireland visited the Fulton Street Prayer Meeting to see what it was all about. "We have connected with our synod 500 churches and congregations," they said, "And we have a strong desire that the same gracious dispensation which has blessed you here be bestowed upon all our churches at home."

The awakening in Ireland became known as the Ulster Revival of 1859. Meetings often lasted into the morning hours, and in the town of Conor, six of nine saloons were closed because of the revival. Similar awakenings were reported in Scotland, Wales and England.

---

[21] McDow & Reid, *FireFall*, 268.

# All Segments of Society Impacted

The Prayer Revival had a profound impact on all segments of the society. It was a common sight for businesses to have signs on their doors informing customers that they were closed for the noon prayer meeting.

Newspapers carried regular reports of the revival and its progress. The editors of the daily *New York Herald* carried a regular section called "Revival Extras" by which they informed their readers of the latest news concerning the revival.

One Chicago newspaper carried a report which shows the impact the revival was having on the society at large. It read,

> So far as the effects of the present religious movement are concerned, they are apparent to all. They are to be seen in every walk of life, to be felt in every place of society. The merchant, the farmer, the mechanic—all who have been within their influence—have been incited to better things; to a more orderly and honest way of life.[22]

The revival had begun with a simple layman who did not claim any special gift or calling, and the revival continued apart from the guidance of the ordained clergy. Finney, who was ordained with the Congregational Church, wrote,

---

[22] *America's Great Revivals* (Minneapolis: Bethany Fellowship, n.d.), 64-65

It was carried on to a large extent through lay influence, so much so as almost to throw the ministers into the shade.[23]

This was a profound expression of New Testament Christianity which knew of no formal distinction between "laity" and a professionalized "clergy." "Laity" comes from the Greek word *laos* that is translated "people" in the New Testament. Paul, Peter, John and Barnabas, though obvious leaders, are all part of the *laos*, *i.e.*, the people of God. In the New Testament Church, the *laos* (people) are all filled with the Spirit and equipped to carry out the work of the ministry.

This New Testament reality was expressed in a very profound way in the Great Prayer Revival. One of the people profoundly impacted in this revival was a young D. L. Moody who later became the nation's most successful evangelist. Interestingly, Moody chose not to be ordained, influenced, no doubt, by what he saw and experienced in the Prayer Revival.

## The Prayer Awakening Continues

Although this great Prayer Revival is often identified with the years 1857-58, it did not suddenly cease after those dates. Those dates merely identify the revival at its height and period of its greatest impact.

The spirit of prayer actually continued and carried over into the Civil War. As we shall see in the following

---

[23] Finney, *An Autobiography*, 442.

chapter, prayer played a primary role in ending the war and keeping the nation from being torn apart.

# Chapter 5

# Prayer Saves the Nation

*When everyone seemed panic-stricken, I went to my room and got down on my knees before Almighty God and prayed. Soon a sweet comfort crept into my soul that God Almighty had taken the whole business into His own hands.* - Abraham Lincoln

Some have suggested that the Prayer Revival of 1857-58 was an outpouring of God's mercy preceding national judgment for the institutional sin of slavery—that it was God giving the nation an opportunity to deal with this sin and thereby avoid the coming judgment.

The slavery issue was not dealt with and on April 12, 1861 the first shot of the Civil War was fired, igniting the costliest war in American history, and the only war fought on American soil.

## The Greatest Tragedy in American History

There was great loss on all fronts, but none so great as the loss of human life. Estimates of the loss of life range from 625,000 to over 700,000 soldiers and an unknown number of civilians. The magnitude of the loss is amplified by the fact that the United States population at the time was only 31 million.

By way of comparison, in WWII 50,000 American soldiers lost their lives. In the conflicts in Iraq and Afghanistan less than 10,000 Americans have died. More lives were lost in the Civil War than in all wars combined from the American Revolution through the Korean Conflict.

It was truly a devastating time. Weeping could be heard in homes throughout America. In many homes both father and sons were missing. Hardly a family could be found that had not lost multiple family members.

The nation was devastated only a few years after the Great Prayer Revival. However, there is evidence that the spirit of prayer continued during the war and, no doubt, preserved the populace and the nation from utter ruin.

## Mercy Mixed with Judgment

Giardeau, the pastor from South Carolina, believed the revival was sent to prepare the hearts of so many who would soon lose their lives in the Civil War. He described the revival as "the Lord's mercy in gathering His elect for the great war that was soon to sweep so many of them into eternity."

Others would emphasize that the revival was God's way of strengthening and preparing the nation for the terrible time of suffering it would endure through the Civil War. In their excellent book, *FIREFALL: How God Has Shaped History Through Revivals*, McDow and Reid write,

> The Prayer Revival laid the foundation to give spiritual resources that would help the nation survive this conflict. Roy Fish notes that one of the major functions of the great awakening of 1858

had to do with its preparation of the country for its fratricidal war which clouded the horizon."[24]

## Prayer Continues During the War

There is no doubt that the impact of the prayer revival did sustain the nation through this difficult time. There are reports of prayer meetings being prominent in both the Northern and Southern armies—a carry-over from the Prayer Revival.

For example, after the commencement of the war, Jefferson Davis called for nine days of prayer and fasting throughout the Confederate states. And when things were not going well for the Union army in the early days of the war, President Lincoln expressed concern that the "rebel soldiers" were praying more fervently than those of the North. The noted historian, Mark A. Noll, says, "Revivals were common in both camps of the Blue and the Gray."[25]

## A National Day of Prayer Changes the Course of the War

With the North suffering one defeat after another and things looking grim for the state of the Union, the U.S. Senate passed a resolution asking the president to proclaim a national day of fasting and prayer.

President Lincoln then designated April 30, 1863 as a national day of humiliation, prayer and the confession of

---

[24] McDow & Reid, *FireFall*, 265.
[25] Mark A Noll, *History of Christianity in the United States and Canada* (Grand Rapids: Eerdmans, 1992), 318.

national sins, which would include the sin of slavery. Because of the power of his proclamation, the complete text is included here.

*Whereas, the Senate of the United States devoutly recognizing the Supreme Authority and just Government of Almighty God in all the affairs of men and of nations, has, by a resolution, requested the President to designate and set apart a day for national prayer and humiliation:*

*And whereas, it is the duty of nations as well as of men to own their dependence upon the overruling power of God, to confess their sins and transgressions in humble sorrow yet with assured hope that genuine repentance will lead to mercy and pardon, and to recognize the sublime truth, announced in the Holy Scriptures and proven by all history: that those nations only are blessed whose God is Lord:*

*And, insomuch as we know that, by His divine law, nations like individuals are subjected to punishments and chastisement in this world, may we not justly fear that the awful calamity of civil war, which now desolates the land, may be but a punishment inflicted upon us for our presumptuous sins to the needful end of our national reformation as a whole people?*

*We have been the recipients of the choicest bounties of Heaven. We have been preserved these many years in peace and prosperity. We have grown in numbers, wealth and power as no other nation has ever grown.*

*But we have forgotten God. We have forgotten the gracious Hand which preserved us in peace and multiplied and enriched and strengthened us; and we have vainly imagined, in the deceitfulness of our hearts, that all these blessings were produced by some superior wisdom and virtue of our own.*

*Intoxicated with unbroken success, we have become too self-sufficient to feel the necessity of redeeming and preserving grace, too proud to pray to the God that made us!*

*It behooves us then to humble ourselves before the offended Power, to confess our national sins and to pray for clemency and forgiveness.*

*Now, therefore, in compliance with the request and fully concurring in the view of the Senate, I do, by this proclamation, designate and set apart Thursday, the 30th day of April, 1863, as a day of national humiliation, fasting and prayer.*

*And I do hereby request all the people to abstain on that day from their ordinary secular pursuits, and to unite, at their several places of public worship and their respective homes, in keeping the day holy to the Lord and devoted to the humble discharge of the religious duties proper to that solemn occasion.*

*All this being done, in sincerity and truth, let us then rest humbly in the hope authorized by the Divine teachings, that the united cry of the nation will be heard on high and answered with blessing no less than the pardon of our national sins and the restoration of our now divided and suffering country to its former happy condition of unity and peace.*

*In witness whereof, I have hereunto set my hand and caused the seal of the United States to be affixed. By the President: Abraham Lincoln.*

## Lincoln's Prayer of Faith

Because the influence of the Great Prayer Awakening was still fresh in the minds of the people, they responded *en masse* to Lincoln's call to prayer. And after this national day of repentance and prayer, there was an almost immediate turn of the war in favor of the North--but not before a severe test of faith.

The following June, a confident General Robert E. Lee led 76,000 Confederate troops north into Union territory, *i.e.*, into Pennsylvania. The populace was terrified and there was much panic. Lincoln, however, having been impacted by the Prayer Revival, found solace in prayer. He said,

> When everyone seemed panic-stricken, I went to my room and got down on my knees before Almighty God and prayed. Soon a sweet comfort crept into my soul that God Almighty had taken the whole business into His own hands.

The Confederate forces were defeated at Gettysburg on July 3 and that battle proved to be the turning point for the war. It was also the occasion of Lincoln's "Gettysburg Address," one of the most significant speeches ever delivered by a national leader.

Some would say the victory at Gettysburg was coincidental, but the change came on heels of the national day of repentance, prayer and fasting. One writer surmised that the North did not win the Civil War, but that prayer won the war.

## Whose Side Are We On?

During the war, there were bold claims from both sides that God was on their side and defending their cause. Lincoln expressed a different perspective. When a minister from the North expressed to the president his hope that "the Lord is on our side," Lincoln replied,

> I am not at all concerned about that . . . but it is my constant anxiety and prayer that I and this nation should be on the Lord's side."[26]

## The War Ends • The Healing Continues

For all practical purposes, the war ended in the spring of 1865, when Robert E. Lee and the last major Confederate army surrendered at the Appomattox Courthouse in Virginia to Ulysses S. Grant on April 9. Over the next few months smaller units throughout the South laid down their arms and the bloodiest four years in American history came to an end.

It was from this era and out of this environment of both prayer and hostilities that the Negro spiritual came forth that included the repeated phrase, "Ain't gonna study war no more." It captured the deepest feelings of many

---

[26] Noll, 323.

who longed for peace and a sense of God's blessing once
again on the nation.

Gonna lay down my burdens,
Down by the riverside,
Down by the riverside, down by the riverside.
Gonna lay down my burdens,
Down by the riverside.
Ain't gonna study war no more.

Gonna sit down with Jesus,
Down by the riverside,
Down by the riverside, down by the riverside.
Gonna sit down with Jesus,
Down by the riverside.
Ain't gonna study war no more.

# Chapter 6

# It Can Happen Again
# If My People . . .

*If My people who are called by My name will humble themselves, and pray and seek My face, and turn from their wicked ways, then I will hear from heaven, and will forgive their sin and heal their land.* – II Chronicles 7:14

America is now facing another great crisis, perhaps even more daunting than the Civil War. This is so because the moral and religious pillars of support that were in place at that time have been removed.

## What is Different Now

At the time of the Civil War, Biblical Christianity was still the accepted belief of the masses, including the politicians. Even if many were indifferent to the message of Christianity, and did not live up to its vision, it was there as an accepted standard towards which the masses could be called.

At the time of the Civil War, America's Christian history was still in place and the faith of the Founders was general knowledge. Despite the institutional and personal sins of the nation, Christianity was a present, positive and moral force. Even though Southerners sought to defend the institution of slavery, they were always on the defensive because of this Christian influence.

Today, however, those Christian values that ended slavery and appealed to the very best in our nature have been eroded by politically-correct politicians and secularists who have re-written our history and re-interpreted our Constitution. Prayer and Bible reading are banned from public schools and crosses and Christian symbols have been removed from government facilities.

Religious liberty has come under attack on a widespread basis and left-wing bureaucrats and politicians are hard at work destroying every vestige of Christian influence from America's public life.

In the face of this onslaught, the church has seemed feckless. Despite our mega churches, large conferences, talk of taking cities for God and claims of apostolic restoration, the culture has continued to decline, becoming crude, crass and barbaric.

Same-sex marriage was legalized in 2015 and brought with it an increased animus toward Bible-believing Christians. At the same time, Islam has continued to increase in numbers and influence while the percentage of Christians in America has continued to drop--from 86% in the 1990s to 73 % today.

## We Have a Window of Opportunity

By 2016, things were looking grim for Bible-believing Christians in America. Government hostility was on the rise and the presidential candidate whom the experts said would win, had referred to Bible-believing Christians as "deplorable."

God, however, intervened. The American church was given a reprieve and a window of opportunity by the election of Donald Trump, who despite his flaws, fights for religious liberty and the right of Christians to live out their faith in the marketplace. He was elected because millions of concerned Christians prayed and turned out to vote.

This turn of events, that surprised all the experts, presents an opportunity that we must not allow to slip away. We must maximize this moment God has graciously given us. As Jesus said in John 9:7, *I must work the works of Him who sent me while it is day. The night is coming when no one can work.*

## If My People . . .

It is of utmost importance that we realize that even though evangelical Christians helped elect a president, the Awakening that will save America will not arise from a political process or party. The next Great Awakening will not begin at the White House, but at God's House. The change we so desperately need will come when Christians meet, not in Washington D.C, but in II Chronicles 7:14.

The promise of a national healing in II Chronicles 7:14 begins with the condition, *If My people . . .* Notice that God did not say, "if the king," or "if the judges." He said, *If My people . . ..* This means that America's future is in our hands.

This was powerfully illustrated by an event described by Dr. Billye Brim in her book, *First of All & the Awakenings.*

She tells how, in 1979, she and about forty others had gathered to pray for the upcoming elections and for Israel.

As they "prayed up a storm" for the approaching election, the Spirit of God suddenly fell on her in a way that stunned her. Words came with such power, she said, "It was almost like I had to speak them or die." She found herself declaring,

> One thing will save America.
> And it is not the election.
> It is an Awakening to God.
> One thing will avail for Israel and the nations.
> It is an Awakening to God.[27]

She said, "These words shook us. Silenced us. Even rebuked us." They suddenly realized the reality of II Chronicles 7:14. Unless the people of God wake up and fulfill those conditions for a national awakening and healing, it won't matter who is in the White House or on the Supreme Court.

Yes, the time has come for the American church to awaken. I Peter 4:17 says, *For the time has come for judgment to begin at the house of God.* And in II Corinthians 13:5, Paul exhorted the Corinthian church,

> *Examine yourselves as to whether you are in the faith. Test yourselves. Do you not know yourselves, that Jesus Christ is in you?—unless indeed you are disqualified.*

---

[27] Dr. Billye Brim, *First Things First & the Awakenings* (Joplin, MO: Billye Brim Ministries, 2017), 8.

# Humble Themselves and Pray

As believers, we carry out this admonition of self-judgement, not by an unhealthy, navel-gazing introspection, but by inviting the Holy Spirit to search our hearts and then making the appropriate confession and repentance according to what is revealed.

This is what David did and it earned him the designation from God as, *A man after My own heart* (Acts 13:22). In Psalm 139:23, he prayed,

> *Search me, O God, and know my heart; try me and know my anxieties; and see if there is any wicked way in me, and lead me in the way everlasting.*

This is what George Whitefield did before departing England to preach the gospel in America. Having been ordained with the Church of England, the twenty-three-year old Whitefield shared his plan with the Bishop of London. The bishop replied that he would look favorably upon anyone preaching in America, "If they did not go out of any sinister view."

Those words pierced Whitefield's heart and he later wrote,

> This put me upon enquiry what my motives were in going? And after the strictest examination, my conscience answered, "Not to please any man living upon earth, nor out of any sinister view, but

simply to comply with what I believe to be Thy will, O God, and to promote Thy glory."[28]

In Matthew 5:8, Jesus said, *Blessed are the pure in heart for they shall see God*. Over the next thirty-three years, with a purified heart, Whitefield made seven trips across the Atlantic. He became the primary instrument of God in the First Great Awakening that transformed Colonial America and prepared her for statehood. His tireless labors and impact earned him the title, "America's Spiritual Founding Father."

This is also what happened in a church, described by Charles Finney, during the Second Great Awakening. The leaders of this church opened themselves to the One *who has eyes like a flame of fire*, which penetrate to the very core of our being (Revelation 2:18).

Under the searchlight of the Holy Spirit, they came to realize that in seeking acceptance and approval from society and culture, they had compromised their commitment to Christ. They were humbled and heartbroken at their compromise with the world.

They, therefore, formulated a public statement concerning what they called, "their backsliding and want of a Christian spirit."[29] The statement was submitted to the members of the congregation for their approval and then read before the assembled congregation.

---

[28] George Whitefield, *George Whitefield's Journals* (Carlisle, PA: Banner of Truth Trust, 1960), 82.
[29] Charles G. Finney, *The Original Memoirs of Charles G. Finney*, Garth M. Rosell & Richard A.G. Dupuis, eds. (Grand Rapids: Zondervan, 2002), 163.

As the confession was being read publicly, the entire congregation stood to its feet with many of its members weeping. Finney said that, from that moment on, the revival went forward in power, and the opposition, which had been bitter, was silenced.

## And Seek My Face

Many years ago, a prayer leader told how He heard the Lord say to Him, "Do not seek My hand." Sometime later, during a time of prayer, he heard the Lord say, "Seek My face and I will show you My hand." God's hand represents His power, but His face represents He Himself.

*Seek My face*, is one of the conditions for a national healing that comes immediately after, *humble themselves and pray* (II Chronicles 7:14). To seek the Lord's face means that we seek Him, not for what we can get from Him, but because we want to know Him and understand His heart, ways and purpose.

Sadly, many ministers never get around to seeking God's face. Finney, for example, tells about receiving numerous invitations from churches and pastors wanting revival, but who were unwilling to humble themselves before God and seek His face. They were only interested in His hand—His power—and that for self-serving reasons.

In his *Lectures on Revival* he tells how some wanted revival in order to raise their social status and influence. Others wanted revival to increase the numbers attending their meetings, which in turn would enable them to build new and larger buildings.

Still others wanted revival so that they would feel superior to one or more congregations with whom they felt a sense of competition. All were seeking revival from self-centered motives, and Finney refused their requests. He said,

> When I came to weigh their reasons, I have sometimes found every one of them to be selfish. And God would look upon every one with abhorrence.[30]

When we neglect to humble ourselves and seek His face, *ego* and pride will color and taint everything we do. Even our "revivals" and "worship" will become abominable in God's sight as were the prayers and fasting of the Pharisees.

This was made real to this writer some years ago as I sat on the platform of a well-known ministry and noted a troubling in my spirit during the praise and worship. Outwardly, everything was great. The musicians and singers were superb. The congregation was very enthusiastic, and some danced in the aisles and others waved banners.

As I prayerfully pondered the troubling in my spirit, I heard the Holy Spirit speak in my heart, "Look around," He said, "Who is this for?" As I looked around, the answer became clear. This was for them. They were having fun. They were reveling in their own excellence and feeling proud of their expertise in "worship." They

---

[30] Charles G. Finney, *Revival Lectures* (Grand Rapids: Fleming H. Revell, n.d.), 351.

were more enamored with their act of worship than with the object of worship.

I was then reminded of God's rebuke to Israel for their anthropocentric, self-serving worship. They too had lost their focus on the Almighty and had become centered on themselves. Through the prophet Zechariah, God rebuked them, saying,

> During those seventy years of exile when you fasted and mourned, was it really for Me? And even now in your holy festivals, you don't think about Me but only of pleasing yourselves (Zech. 7:5-6, NLT).

The generation of Israelites, that came out of Egypt did not possess their promised land because they were not interested in God's face. They were only interested in his hand—His acts of power. They wanted God to do stuff for them. They saw God as the *means* for their self-fulfillment.

Moses, however, was not satisfied to just see God's hand. Moses wanted to see His face. Moses wanted to know Him and His ways. God was not a *means* to Moses, God was the *end* and *goal* of life and everything.

Moses, therefore, pleaded with God in Exodus 33;13, *Now therefore, I pray, if I have found grace in Your sight, show me now Your way, that I may know You . . .*. God heard his prayer and many years later, the Psalmist, wrote, *He made known His ways to Moses, His acts to the children of Israel* (Psalm 103:7).

# Then God Will Heal Our Land

II Chronicles 7:14 gives specific conditions for a national healing. Those condition are:

1. Humble yourselves and pray.
2. Seek My face.
3. Turn from your wicked ways.

After listing those conditions, God says, **Then** *I will hear from heaven and will forgive their sin and heal their land.* **Then**, and not before. There are no shortcuts to a Great Awakening that will heal our land.

It is my prayer that we, as American Christians, and Christians of every nation, will humble ourselves before God and repent for distorting revival, church and worship with our selfishness, *ego* and pride. It is my desire that we will begin to seek His face, by seeking to know Him, His heart and His ways.

As we seek His face, He will show us His hand. God will answer with *times of refreshing from the presence of the Lord*, as promised in Acts 3:19. He will forgive our sin and heal our land as promised in II Chronicles 7:14. The land will be healed, and America's God-given destiny will be preserved for the coming generation.

# Chapter 7

# How God Restored
# My Hope for America

In 2010 I had given up hope of America ever seeing another national, spiritual awakening that would impact the culture and stem the tide of secularism, immorality, and false religion that was flooding our land. This state of hopelessness had come about after seeing the culture continuing to decline despite the local and regional revivals of the 1990s.

Revival, you must realize, had been a part of my life as far back as I can remember. I recall my parents taking my brothers and I to the giant tents of the healing revivalists in the 1950s. I had also seen powerful moves of the Holy Spirit in the churches in which I was reared and pastored by my father.

In the 1970s I was exposed for the first time to the writings of Charles G. Finney and my heart was stirred to see transformative revivals such as he described in his Autobiography.

As God led me into higher education, I was able channel this passion for revival into my studies and my doctoral dissertation. Out of these studies came my book, *2000 Years of Charismatic Christianity*, which God has used as an instrument of blessing in many parts of the world.

In August of 1993 as I was walking and praying in Tulsa,

Oklahoma, I heard the Holy Spirit speak in my heart, "A new wave of Holy Spirit outpouring is coming and will continue to the end of the century." It was such a vivid experience that when I returned home, I immediately wrote those words in my calendar, which I still have.

There did come powerful revivals in Toronto, Tulsa, Pensacola, Texas and in many locations throughout the nation and the world. I had hopes that this would be the next Great Awakening that would transform American culture. Sadly, however, the revival never reached that level of influence.

Pride and *ego* intruded. In some situations, "revival" was just a term for a self-serving pursuit of a good time at church. I remember walking out of one so-called revival meeting with my spirit so grieved that I said to myself, "If this is revival, I want nothing to do with it."

As I observed the American culture becoming more crude and ungodly, I gave up hope that America would ever see another Great Awakening that would impact the culture and stem the tide of secularism, immorality and false religions flooding the land.

This all changed, however, one hot July day in 2010. Without any expectation of any such thing happening, God suddenly confronted me with hope. It began with a two-hour drive from Tulsa to Kingfisher, OK where I was scheduled to preach the next day in a Sunday morning service.

As I pulled onto the highway, it seemed that I was suddenly enveloped in God's presence. At the same time, my heart and mind began to be flooded with thoughts of hope and faith that America "could" see another Great Awakening.

As I drove along the highway, I was hardly aware of my surroundings as my heart overflowed with excitement at what I was seeing and experiencing. By the time I reached the hotel where I would be staying, I could hardly wait to get settled in the room with my notebook computer and begin writing down the thoughts and ideas that were still flooding my mind.

This experience lasted far into the night as I sat on the bed, wrote, prayed and praised God. Two main points were indelibly inscribed on my heart from that experience.

1. My hope was restored that America "could" see another Great Awakening.

2. I saw for the first time that there was a direct bearing of the First Great Awakening on the founding of America.

Out of that experience came the book, *America's Revival Heritage*. When it sold out, I began doing an edit and adding new research. In the process, I suddenly realized that I had another book and *Pilgrims and Patriots* came forth and was published in 2016.

Out of this experience, and based on the books, I developed a PowerPoint presentation that I call "America Reawakening." It consists of three PowerPoint presentations that document America's Christian birth out of a great, Spiritual awakening.

During the above experience, I was very aware that God was saying that America "could," not "would," see another Great Awakening. In other words, it is not a done deal. It can happen, *if My people* . .

Will you join me and thousands of others in fulfilling these conditions for another Great Awakening?

# About the Author

Dr. Eddie L. Hyatt is a seasoned minister of the Gospel with over 45 years of ministerial experience as a pastor, Bible teacher and Professor of Theology. He holds the Doctor of Ministry from Regent University as well as the Master of Divinity and a Master of Arts from Oral Roberts University. He has authored several books, including *2000 Years of Charismatic Christianity*, which is used as a textbook in colleges and seminaries around the world. Eddie's current passion is to call America back to its founding principles of freedom and Spiritual awakening. He is doing this through his writings and by conducting "America Reawakening" events in which he shows how America was birthed out of a Christian worldview and spiritual awakening. He resides in Grapevine, TX with his wife, Dr. Susan Hyatt, where they are establishing the Int'l Christian Women's Hall of Fame and Ministry Center. If you would like to contact him, his email address is dreddiehyatt@gmail.com. His website address is www.eddiehyatt.com.

For discounts on bulk orders of this book, send an email to dreddiehyatt@gmail.com.

## Other Books by Drs. Eddie & Susan Hyatt

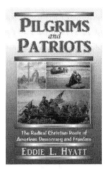  

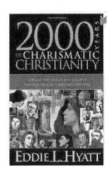 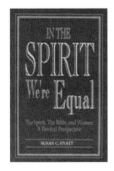 

These and other materials are available from Amazon and from www.eddiehyatt.com and www.godswordtowomen.org.

# AMERICA REAWAKENING

Winston Churchill said, "The greatest advances in civilization have come when we have learned the lessons of history." This is an inspiring, 3-Session PowerPoint Presentation that documents how our nation was birthed out of prayer and a great, spiritual awakening. This knowledge is critical, for as George Orwell said, "Whoever controls the past controls the future."

## TRANSFORMED BY SPIRITUAL AWAKENING

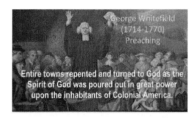 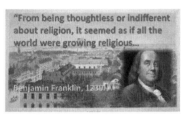

## A NATION IS BORN

## IT'S TIME FOR A REAWAKENING

 If you would like to sponsor an "America Reawakening" event for your church, school, or city, contact me at dreddiehyatt@gmail.com.

60898792R00036

Made in the USA
Columbia, SC
19 June 2019